The Catholic Priest

Fr. Michael Muller, C.SS.R.

SENSUS FIDELIUM PRESS
Gastonia, North Carolina

Contents

CHAPTER 1

INTRODUCTORY

WHEN our dear Savior Jesus Christ was living on earth, He was accused of the worst crimes. He was accused by the high-priests and the doctors of the law, to whom it belonged to pronounce who was the Messiah. He was accused before an idolatrous judge, in the presence of all the people. He was treated as a blasphemer, as one possessed by the devil, as a lover of wine, as a destroyer of the Temple, as a seducer of the people, as a rebel, a seditious man, who gave to Himself the title of king, who forbade the payment of tribute to Caesar, and who wished to destroy the Jewish nation. If ever infamous calumny was carried to excess, it was undoubtedly in regard to our divine Savior Jesus Christ, "who knew not sin," who had never uttered a deceitful word, who "did all things well," and who "passed His life in doing good and healing all kinds of infirmities."

Now Jesus Christ continues to live in the hierarchy of the Catholic Church, the Pope, the bishops, and priests. He has made a prediction to His Apostles and their successors, which has come true in all ages, and which will be verified to the end of the world. He said to them: "The servant is not greater than his lord; if they have persecuted me, they will also persecute you." (John xv. 20.) This prediction of our Lord Jesus Christ has been especially verified in our own century. See how the enemies of Jesus Christ have treated, and how they continue still to treat, our holy father Pius IX.; see how they massacred the Archbishop of Paris, and many of his clergy, in cold blood! The Pope! the Pope! The Priest I the Priest! This has ever been the cry of all the wicked, and what fancies has it not conjured up? Some, when they only hear the word "Pope," or "Priest," turn up their eyes in horror, and shrink back as if they had suddenly encountered an evil genius. Others, at the mere sound of the word "Pope," or "Priest," become as rabid as a dog stricken with hydrophobia when he sees water. They grind their teeth, they froth and foam at the mouth, they tremble with rage, and seem as if they would tear into pieces all the popes and priests that have ever lived from Peter to the present day.

Others shake their heads with an air of majesty, as if they would say: "How can we get over the Pope over the hierarchy of the Catholic Church?" Like a divine stigma, the world's hatred is impressed on the brow of the Pope, of the bishops and priests of the Church. The spirit of the world the spirit of falsehood and of negation hates the Pope the Vicar of Christ; it hates all our Lord s true ministers the Catholic bishops and priests with demoniacal hatred. Why? Because they are the palladium of truth, and of public and private morality, the root and bond of charity and of faith.

The spirit of the world hates the Pope, it hates the bishops and priests of the Catholic Church, because they love justice and hate iniquity. But it is for this very reason that they will remain forever; for truth and justice being, in the end, always victorious, the Pope, together with the Catholic bishops and priests, will not cease to bless and to triumph. All the works of the earth have perished; time has obliterated them. The hierarchy of the Catholic Church remains, because the Church remains, and it will endure until the Church passes from her earthly exile to her country in heaven

Human theories and systems have flitted across her path like birds of night, but have vanished; numberless sects have, like so many waves, dashed themselves to froth against this rock, or, recoiling, have been lost in the vast ocean of forgetfulness. Kingdoms and empires that once existed in inimitable worldly grandeur are no more; dynasties have died out and have been replaced by others.

Thrones, scepters, and crowns have withstood the hierarchy of the Church; but, immutable, like God, who laid its foundation, it is the firm, unshaken center round which the weal and woe of nations move weal if they adhere to it woe if they separate from it. If the world takes from the Pope, the bishops, and priests of the Catholic Church, the cross of gold, they will bless the world with one of wood. If necessary, popes, bishops and priests can suffer and die for the welfare of the world, as Jesus suffered and died. The hierarchy of the Catholic Church is immortal.

We cannot but smile when we hear men talk of the downfall of this hierarchy. What could hell and its agents do more than they have already done for its destruction? They have employed tortures for the body, but they could not reach the spirit; they have tried heresy, or the denial of revealed truth, to such an extent that we cannot see room for any new heresy; they have, by the hand of schism, torn whole countries from the unity of the Church; but what she lost on one side of the globe, she gained tenfold on the other. All these have ignominiously failed to verify the prophecies of hell, that "the hierarchy of the Church shall fall."

Look, for instance, at the tremendous effort of the so-called glorious Reformation, together with its twin sister the unbelief of the nineteenth century. Whole legions of church reformers, together with armies of philosophers armed with negation, and a thousand and one systems of paganism, rushed on against the chair of Peter, and swore that the papacy would fall, and with it the whole hierarchy of the Church. Three hundred years are over, and the hierarchy of the Catholic Church is still alive, and, to all appearances, more vigorous than ever. The nations have proved that they can get along very well without reformers, but not without the Pope, the bishops and priests of the Catholic Church. Men are foolish enough to dream of the destruction of the papacy.

Napoleon tried the game, and, from the summit of his empire, walked into exile, whilst his victim, Pius VII., leaving his prison, entered Rome in triumph. A great statesman of France said, not long ago, that those who tried to swallow the papacy, and with it the whole hierarchy of the Church, always died of indigestion. Let the enemies of the Pope, and of the Catholic bishops and priests, beware: if they dash their heads against the rock, they must not be astonished to find them broken.

The whole hierarchy of the Catholic Church is a grand fact in history a fact so great that there would be no history without it a fact permanent, repeating itself perpetually, entering into the concerns of all the nations on the face of the earth, appearing again and again on the records of time, and benefiting, perceived or unperceived, directly or indirectly, socially, morally, and supernaturally, every individual who forms part of the great organism of human society.

Around this hierarchy human society moves like a wheel around its axle; on this hierarchy society depends for its support, its life, its energy, like the planetary system on the sun. This assertion, my dear reader, I hope to make good by showing to you in this little work that the Pope, the bishops and priests are "the light of the world, the salt of the earth, the mediators between God and man, and the best fathers and friends of the people."

Chapter 2

THEY ARE "THE LIGHT OF THE WORLD"

THE great roots of all the evils that press upon society, and make man unhappy, are "THE IGNORANCE OF THE MIND, AND THE DEPRAVITY OF THE WILL." Hence, he who wishes to civilize the world, and thus assist in executing the plans of God s providence, must remove these two great roots of evil by imparting to the mind infallibly the light of truth, and by laying down for the will authoritatively the unchangeable principles of morality. If the hierarchy of the Catholic Church has accomplished in society this twofold task, then has it rendered itself worthy of the praises of all men, and deserves to be called the greatest, the most astonishing, the most divine fact in the history of the world then the hierarchy of the Catholic Church is truly "the light of the world, and the salt of the earth." Look at the world before Christianity. Everywhere the grossest ignorance and immorality prevailed. The true God was hardly known, save in one single corner of the earth, which is to say, in Judea alone; and even there, how very few loved Him! As to the rest of the world, some worshipped the sun, some the brutes, some the very stones, and others again even viler creatures still; nay, many even worshipped the very demons as gods. Everywhere there reigned the night of sin which blinds souls and hides from them the sight of the miserable state in which they are living as enemies of God and condemned to hell. The most degrading vices were extolled even as virtues. The world cried for light. Men could no longer see their way. "Why are we here? Who made us? Whither are we going? Whence the evils in the world? Why have we a thirst for immortality? Why does nothing on earth satisfy us? Why our yearning for perpetual happiness?" Such were the questions that resounded everywhere, in the schools of philosophy, in the forum, in the marketplace, in the temple, at the fireside. No one could answer; and yet the social, domestic and religious happiness of the world was at stake on these questions then as it is now. What remedy could be applied to heal such inveterate evils of the mind and the will? Pagan philosophers, poets and orators, had tried their best to elevate mankind; but they had tried in vain. Then "the light shone into the darkness;" and Jesus Christ was this light, by His divine doctrine and example. St. Peter and the other Apostles and their successors the Roman Catholic bishops and priests became the bearers of this light. More than fifteen hundred years ago there hung in the Catacombs of Rome a lamp shaped in the form of a ship, at whose helm sat St. Peter, steering with one hand, and with the other giving his blessing. On one side of this miniature ship were engraved the words, "Peter dies not," and on the other the words of our dear Savior:" I have prayed for thee." (Luke xxii. 32.)

There could not be a more beautiful symbol of the papacy and the hierarchy of the Catholic Church. This hierarchy is a lamp which illumines all darkness and furnishes us with the brilliant light of truth; the Church is a ship which carries this light safely through the storms of ages to the ends of the earth, bringing with it blessings to the nations, and gathering into its apostolic net, as it sails along, the perishing children of men. And at the helm sits the poor fisherman of Galilee, the Pope, together with his assistants the Catholic bishops and priests directing the course of the vessel, now to this, now to that distressed country, now to this, now to that sorrowing people, to bring them not gold, not silver, but what is infinitely more precious Faith; and with faith, true civilization, based upon the unchangeable principles of supernatural morality, true prosperity, true happiness, and peace on earth and for eternity. One thousand eight hundred and forty-odd years ago, a poor, meanly clad wanderer went to the Capital of the world, the wealthy, magnificent city of Rome. He passes its gates and threads his way unobserved through its populous streets. Oil every side he beholds splendid palaces raised at the expense of down-trodden nationalities; he beholds stately temples dedicated to as many false gods as nations were congregated in Rome; he beholds public baths and amphitheaters devoted to pleasure and to cruelty; he beholds statues, monuments, and triumphal arches raised to the memory of blood-thirsty tyrants.

He passes warriors and senators, beggars and cripples, effeminate and dissolute women, gladiators and slaves, merchants and statesmen, orators and philosophers, all classes, all ranks, all conditions of men of every language and color under the sun. Everywhere he sees a maddening race for pleasure, everywhere the impression of luxury, everywhere the full growth of crime, side by side with indescribable suffering, diabolical cruelty, and barbarity. And this poor, meanly clad wanderer, was St. Peter. Oh! how the noble heart of the poor fisherman of Galilee must have bled when he observed the empire of Satan so supreme when he witnessed the shocking licentiousness of the temple and the homestead, when he saw the fearful degradation of woman groaning under the load of her own infamy, when he saw the heart-rending inhumanity which slew the innocent babes, and threw them into the Tiber, when he saw how prisoners of war, slaves, soldiers, were trained for bloody fights, and entered the arena of the amphitheater and strove whole days to strangle one another, for the special entertainment of the Roman people. Here, then, was to be the scene of his labors: into this foul mass, into this carcass of a rotten society, St. Peter was come to infuse a new life, to lay the foundation of a new Rome, a Rome which, instead of paganism and depravity, would convey the truth and the blessing of Christian virtues to the farthermost ends of the earth. When Peter, the first Pope, came to Rome, that city was the condensation of all the idolatry, all the oppression, all the injustice, all the immoralities, of the world; for the world was centered in Rome. Hence the work of Peter was the type of what his successors and their fellow-laborers in the vineyard of the Lord the Catholic bishops and priests would do for the world. Peter laid his hand to the plough and never once looked back. For twenty-five years he struggled, and succeeded in establishing, in the very midst of this center of every excess of which the human mind and the human heart could be guilty, a congregation of Christians, to whom St. Paul could address an epistle, and in it state that the far fame of their faith had already spread over the whole world. "I give thanks to my God through Jesus Christ for you all, because your faith is spoken of in the whole world." (Rom. i. 8, xvi. 19.)

The foundation of a new world had been laid by the first Pope and cemented by his own blood. Since then, Pope has succeeded Pope in spite of persecution and death, in spite of the opposition of pagan philosophy and of pagan intrigue, of pagan hate and of pagan enmity. It was through the Popes and their fellow- laborers the Catholic priests that Christianity, till at the end of the third century, covered the whole then known world. The Capitoline temple, and with it the many shrines of idolatry, the golden house of Nero, and with-it Roman excess and Roman cruelty, the throne of the Caesars, and with-it Roman oppression and Roman injustice, had all passed away. And there stood the Rome of the Fathers of the Church, the Rome which was yet to do such wonders in the world. Two hundred and fifty-eight Popes have, till now, succeeded each other in the See of Peter. Of these, seventy-seven are honored by the Church as saints, and twenty-seven have, in imitation of Peter, sealed their work with their blood." And the light shone into the dark ness." Pope after Pope, the principal bearers of the light of the true faith, sent forth to the nations bishops and missionaries, full of the spirit of self-sacrifice, solely devoted to their great task ; and year after year new tribes, new nations, were gained for Christ by the constant labors and hardships of the priests of the Catholic Church. Thus St. Austin brought the light of faith to England, St. Patrick to Ireland, St. Boniface to Germany. The Frieslanders, the Moravians, the Prussians, the Swedes, the Picts, the Scots, the Franks, and hundreds of others, were brought to the bosom of the Church through the preaching and labors of the bishops and priests of the Roman Catholic Church. Driven from one country, their influence was made to act on another. When Solisman, the Sultan, threatened to wipe out Christianity from Europe, Roman Catholic bishops and priests went to the East Indies, to China, and Japan. When Europe failed in its fidelity, and listened to the siren voices of heresy, Catholic bishops and priests were sent to the newly discovered continent of America, and to the West Indies.

Gregory XVI devised plans for missions to the interior of Africa, missions which are working wonders yet. This great work of enlightening the world the Popes accomplished more particularly by those astonishing organizations called Religious Orders, all of which depend for their existence on the approbation of the Holy See. It was the great Pope Gregory I, who, a monk himself, gave, by his example, his dignity, his decrees, and institutions, firmness and stability to the monastic life of the West. True wisdom rests for its support on the principles of Faith. Hence the first aim of these religious orders was to spread the light of faith. With what success they did this, we all know. But there was another thing they did: they civilized the countries to which the Papacy had sent them. In the pagan world, education was an edifice built up on the principles of slavery. The motto was," Odi profanum vulgus ciarceo." Education was the privilege of the aristocracy. The great mass of people was studiously kept in ignorance of the treasures of the mind. This state of things was done away with by the Papacy when it established the monastic institutions of the West. The whole of Europe was soon covered with schools, not only for the wealthy, but for the poorest even of the poor. Yes, education was systematized, and an emulation was created for learning, such as the world had never seen before. Italy, Germany, France, England, and Spain had their universities; but side by side with these, their colleges, gymnasiums, parish and village, schools, as numerous as the churches and monasteries, which the efforts of the Holy See had scattered with lavish hand over the length and breadth of the land. And where was the source of all this light? I answer, in Rome. For when the barbarian hordes poured down upon Europe from the Caspian Mountains, it was the Popes who saved civilization. They collected, in the Vatican, the manuscripts of the ancient authors, gathered from all parts of the earth at enormous expense. The barbarians, who destroyed everything by fire and sword, had already advanced as far as Rome. Attila, who called himself the scourge of God, stood before its walls; there was no emperor, no pretorian guard, no legions present to save the ancient Capital of the world. But there was a Pope Leo I. And

Leo went forth, and by entreaties, and threats of God's displeasure, induced the dreaded king of the Huns to retire. Scarcely had Attila retired, before Genseric, king of the Vandals, made his appearance, invited by Eudoxia, the empress, to the plunder of Rome. Leo met him and obtained from him the lives and the honor of the Romans, and the sparing of the public monuments which adorned the city in such numbers. Thus, Leo the Great saved Europe from barbarism. To the name of Leo, I might add those of Gregory I., Sylvester II, Gregory XIII, Benedict XIV, Julius III, Paul III, Leo X, Clement VIII, John XX, and a host of others, who must be looked upon as the preservers of science and the arts, even amid the very fearful torrent of barbarism that was spreading itself, like an inundation, over the whole of Europe. The principle of the hierarchy of the Church has ever been this: "By the knowledge of Divine things, and the guidance of an infallible teacher, the human mind must gain certainty in regard to the sublimest problems, the great questions of life: by them the origin, the end, the norm and limit of man s activity must be made known, for then alone can he venture fearlessly upon the sphere of human efforts, and human developments, and human science." And, truly, science has never gained the ascendancy outside of the Church that it has always held in the Church. And what I say of science I also say of the arts. I say it of architecture, of sculpture, and of painting. I need only point to the Basilica of Peter, to the museums and libraries of Rome. It is to Rome the youthful artist always turns his steps, in order to drink in, at the monuments of art and of science, the genius and inspiration he seeks for in vain in his own country. He feels, only too keenly, that railroads and telegraphs, steamships and power-looms, banking-houses and stock companies, though good and useful institutions, are not the mothers of genius, nor the schools of inspiration; and therefore he leaves his country, and goes to Rome, and there feasts on the fruits gathered by the hands of St. Peter's successors, and then returns home with a name which will live for ages in the memory of those who have learned to appreciate the true and the beautiful.

It is thus that the Popes, and bishops and priests have accomplished the first magnificent work of enlightening society. They have shed the light of Faith over the East and the West, over the North and the South, and with the faith they have established the principles of true science on their natural basis. They have imparted education to the masses, wherever they were left free to adopt their own, and untrammeled by civil interference. They have fostered and protected, yes, gathered around themselves the arts and the sciences, and today, if all the libraries, and all the museums, and all the galleries of art in the world were destroyed. Rome alone would possess quite enough to supply the want, as it did in former ages, when others supplied themselves by plundering Rome. The depravity of man shows itself in the constant endeavor to shake off the restraint placed by law and duty upon his will; and to this we must ascribe the licentiousness which has at all times afflicted society. Passion acknowledges no law, and spares neither rights nor conventions; where it has the power, it exercises it to the advantage of self, and to the detriment of social order. The Church is by its very constitution Catholic, and hence looks upon all men as brothers of the same family. She acknowledges not the natural right of one man over another, and hence her Catholicity lays a heavy restraint upon all the efforts of self-love, and curbs with a mighty hand the temerity of those who would destroy the harmony of life implied in the idea of Catholicity.

One of the first principles of all social happiness is, that before the law of nature, and before the face of God, all men are equal. This principle is based on the unity of the human race, the origin of all men from one common father. If we study the History of Paganism, we find that all heathen nations overturned this great principle, since we find among all heathen nations the evil of Slavery. Prior to the coming of Christ, the great majority of men were looked upon as a higher development of the animal, as animated instruments which might be bought and sold, given away and pawned; which might be tormented, maltreated, or murdered; as beings, in a word, for whom the idea of right, duty, pity, mercy, and law had no existence. Who can read, without a feeling of intense horror, the accounts left us of the treatment of their slaves by the Romans? There was no law that could restrain in the least the wantonness, the cruelty, the licentious excess of the master, who, as master, possessed the absolute right to do with his slaves whatsoever he pleased. To remove this stain of slavery has ever been the aim of the Popes, bishops, and priests. "Since the Savior and Creator of the world," says Pope Gregory I, in his celebrated decree, "wished to become man, in order, by grace and liberty, to break the chains of our slavery, it is right and good to bestow again upon man, whom nature has permitted to be born free, but whom the law of nations has brought under the yoke of slavery, the blessing of their original liberty." Through all the Middle Ages called by Protestants the dark ages of the world the echo of these words of Gregory I, is heard, and in the 13th century Pope Pius II could say, "Thanks to God, and the Apostolic See, the yoke of slavery does no longer disgrace any European nation." Since then, slavery was again introduced into Africa, and the newly-discovered regions of America, and again the Popes, bishops and priests raised their voices in the interests of liberty, from Pius II to Pius VII, who, even at the time Napoleon had robbed him of his liberty, and held him captive in a foreign land, became the defender of the negro, to Gregory XVI who, on the third of November 1839, insisted in a special Bull on the abolition of the slave trade, and who spoke in a strain as if he had lived and sat side by side with Gregory I, thirteen hundred years before. But here let us observe, that not only the vindication of liberty for all, not only the abolition of slavery, but the very mode of action followed in this matter by the Popes, bishops and priests, has gained for themselves immortal honor, and the esteem of all good men. When the Church abolished slavery in any country where it existed, the Popes, bishops, and priests did not compel masters, by harshness or threats, to manumit their slaves; they did not bring into action the base intrigues, the low chicanery, the canting hypocrisy of modern statesmen; they did not raise armies, and send them into the lands of their masters to burn and to pillage, to lay waste and to destroy; they did not slaughter, by their schemes, over a million of free men and another million of slaves; they did not make widows and orphans without numbers; they did not impoverish the land, and lay upon their subjects burdens which would crush them into very dust. Nothing of all this. That is not the way in which the Church abolished slavery. The Popes sent bishops and priests into those countries where slavery existed, to enlighten the minds of the masters, and convince them that slaves were men, and consequently had souls, like other people, too. The Popes, bishops, and priests infused into the hearts of masters a deep love for Jesus Christ, and consequently a deep love for souls. The Popes, bishops and priests taught masters to look upon their slaves as created by the same God, redeemed by the same Jesus Christ, destined for the same glory. The consequence was, that the relations of slave and master became the relations of brother to brother; the master began to love his slave, and to ameliorate his condition, till, at last, forced by his own acknowledged principles, he granted to him his liberty. Thus, it was that slavery was abolished by the preaching of the Popes, bishops, and priests. The great barrier to all the healthy, permanent, and free development of nations was thus broken down; the blessings, the privileges of society, were made equally attainable by the masses, and ceased to be the special monopoly of a few, who, for the most part, had nothing to recommend them except their wealth.

But even though the Popes have abolished slavery from Christian society, the female portion of our race would always have sunk back into a new slavery, had not the Popes entered the breach for the protection of the Unity, the sanctity, the Indissolubility of matrimony. In the midst of the barbarous ages, during which the conqueror and warrior swayed the scepter of empire, and kings and petty tyrants acknowledged no other right but that of force, it was the privilege of the Popes, and their honor, to oppose themselves and their authority like a wall of brass to the sensuality and the passions of the mighty ones of the earth, and to stand forth as the protectors of innocence and outraged virtue, as the champions of the rights of woman, against the wanton excesses of tyrannical husbands, by enforcing, in their full seventy, the laws of Christian marriage. If Christian Europe is not covered with harems, if polygamy has never gained a foothold in Europe, if, with the indissolubility and sanctity of matrimony, the palladium of European civilization has been saved from destruction, it is all owing to the Popes, the bishops, and priests. "If the Popes" says the Protestant Von Miller, "if the Popes could hold up no other merit than that which they gained by protecting monogamy against the brutal lusts of those in power, notwithstanding bribes, threats, and persecutions, that alone would render them immortal for all future ages." And how had they to battle till they had gained this merit? What sufferings had they to endure, what trials to undergo?

When King Lothair, in the 9th century, repudiated his lawful wife in order to live with a concubine, Pope Nicholas I. at once took upon himself the defense of the rights and of the honor of the unhappy wife. All the arts of an intriguing policy were applied, but Nicholas remained unshaken; threats were used, but Nicholas remained firm. At last, the king's brother, Louis II, appears with an army before the walls of Rome, in order to compel the Pope to yield. It is useless Nicholas swerves not from the line of duty. Rome is besieged; the priests and people are maltreated and plundered; sanctuaries are desecrated; the cross is torn clown and trampled underfoot, and, in the midst of these scenes of blood and sacrilege, Nicholas flies to the Church of St. Peter; there he is besieged by the arm of the Emperor for two clays and two nights: left without food or drink, he is willing to die of starvation on the tomb of St. Peter, rather than yield to a brutal tyrant, and sacrifice the sanctity of Christian marriage, the law of life of Christian society. And the perseverance of Nicholas I was crowned with victory. He had to contend against a licentious king, who was tired of restraint; against an emperor, who with an army at his heels, came to enforce his brother's unjust demands; against two councils of venal bishops, the one at Metz, the other at Aix-la-Chapelle, who had sanctioned the scandals of the adulterous monarch. Yet, with all this opposition, and the suffering it cost him, the Pope succeeded in procuring the acknowledgment of the rights of an injured woman. And during succeeding ages we find Gregory V carrying on a similar combat against King Eobert, and Urban II against King Philip of France. In the 13th century, Philip Augustus, mightier than his predecessors, set to work all the levers of power, in order to move the Pope to divorce him from his wife Ingelburgis. Hear the noble answer of the great Innocent III: "Since, by the grace of God, we have the firm and unshaken will never to separate ourselves from Justice and Truth, neither moved by petitions, nor bribed by presents, neither induced by love, nor intimidated by hate, we will continue to go on in the royal path, turning neither to the right nor to the left; and we judge without any respect to persons, since God Himself does not respect persons."

After the death of his first wife, Isabella, Philip Augustus wished to gain the favor of Denmark by marrying Ingelburgis. The union had hardly been solemnized when he wished to be divorced from her. A council of venal bishops assembled at Compiegne and annulled his lawful marriage. The queen, poor woman, was summoned before her Judges, and the sentence was read and translated to her. She could not speak the language of France, so her only cry was" Rome!" And Rome heard her cry of distress, and carne to her rescue. Innocent III needed the alliance of France, in the troubles in which he was engaged with Germany; Innocent III needed the assistance of France, for the Crusade; yet Innocent III sent Peter of Capua as Legate to France; a Council is convoked by the Legate of the Pope; Philip refuses to appear, in spite of the summons, and the whole of the kingdom of Philip is placed under interdict. Philip's rage knows no bounds: bishops are banished, his lawful wife is imprisoned, and the king vents his rage on the clergy of France. The barons at last appeal against Philip to the sword. The king complains to the Pope of the harshness of the Legate, and when Innocent only confirms the sentence of the Legate, the king exclaims, "Happy Saladin; he had no Pope!" Yet the king was forced to obey. When he asked the barons assembled in council, "What must I do?" their answer was: "Obey the Pope; put away Agnes and restore Ingelburgis." And, thanks to the severity of Innocent III, Philip repudiated the concubine, and restored Ingelburgis to her rights, as wife and queen. Hear what the Protestant Hurter says, in his life of Innocent: "If Christianity has not been thrown aside as a worthless creed, into some isolated corner of the world; if it has not, like the sects of India, been reduced to a mere theory; if its European vitality has outlived the voluptuous effeminacy of the East, it is due to the watch-fill severity of the Roman Pontiffs; to their increasing care to maintain the principles of authority in the Church."

As often as we look to England, that land of perfidy and deceit, we are reminded of the words of Innocent III. to Philip Augustus. We see Clement using them as his principles in his conduct towards the royal brute Henry VIII. Catherine of Aragon, the lawful wife of Henry, had been repudiated by her disgraceful husband, and it was again to Rome she appealed for protection. Clement remonstrates with Henry. The monarch calls the Pope hard names. Clement repeats, "Thou shalt not commit adultery!" Henry threatens to tear England from the Church; he does it; still Clement insists, "Thou shalt not commit adultery!" Fisher and More go to bleed out their life at Tyburn; still the Pope repeats, "Thou shalt not commit adultery!" The firmness of the Pope cost England's loss to the Church. It cost the Pope bitter tears, and he prayed to Heaven not to visit on the people of England the crimes of the despot; he prayed for the conversion of the nation; but sacrifice the sanctity, the indissolubility of matrimony, that he could never do abandon helpless woman to the brutality of men who were tired of the restraints of morality no, that the Pope could never permit. If the Court, if the palace of the domestic hearth refused shelter, Rome was always open, a refuge to injured and down-trodden innocence. "One must obey God more than man."

This has ever been the language of the Popes, of the bishops and priests, whenever there was question of defending the laws of God against the powers of the earth; and in thus defending the laws of God, they protected against outrage the personal dignity, the moral liberty, and the intellectual freedom of man. "Because there was a Pope," says a Protestant historian, "there could not any longer be a Tiberius in Europe, and the direction of the religious and spiritual welfare of man was withdrawn from the hands of royalty." Because there were Popes, the will of Caesar could not any longer be substituted for law; for the Popes made the Gospel the law-book of the nations. Now the Gospel teaches that all power comes from God, that from God the sovereign derives his power, to rule in justice and equity for the welfare of his subjects, and that the subjects are bound to obey their rules for conscience's sake. Hence, adopting the great principle of action, the Popes have at all times condemned the spirit of rebellion, and have anathematized those principles, those factions, those organizations whose aim is, and has always been, to overturn authority and to substitute anarchy in the place of the harmony of legitimate government. In conformity with this rule of action the Popes Clement XII., Benedict XIV, Pius VII, Leo XII, Gregory XVI, and Pius IX, have condemned secret societies, whose object is the overthrow of civil and religious government. But at the same time that the Popes required subjects' obedience to their lawful governments, they have ever defended subjects against the abuse of power, or against the tyranny of unjust rulers. In pagan times it had the appearance as if the people existed for the sovereign, and not the sovereign for the people; but in the days and in the countries where the spiritual supremacy of the Pope was acknowledged by rulers, the pagan idea had necessarily to disappear, for the Popes gave the princes to understand that they existed for the people, and not the people for them.

Viewed in this light, what a magnificent spectacle does the Catholic Church present to our admiration, and how does the honest heart of down-trodden nationality yearn that these happy days may once more return! Taken mostly from the middle classes, sometimes even from the humblest ranks of society, the Popes ascended the chair of Peter. And these men, who had been the sons of artisans and mechanics, but who had, by their virtue and talent, gained a merit which neither wealth nor a noble pedigree could bestow, became the arbiters between nation and nation, between prince and people, always prepared to weld together the chain of broken friendship, and to protect, by their power and authority, the rights of subjects oppressed by tyrannical rulers. It was indeed a blessing for Europe that Nicholas I. could curb, with an iron hand, the tyranny of kings and nobles. It was indeed a blessing, not for Europe alone, but for the world, that there lived a genius on earth in the person of Gregory VII, who knew how to protect the Saxons against the wanton lawlessness of Henry, King of Germany, a monster who ground his subjects remorsely in the dust, and respected neither the sanctity of virginity nor the sacredness of marriage; neither the rights of the Church, nor those of the State; whose very existence seemed to have no other aim but that of the leech, to draw out the blood from the hearts of his unhappy subjects. What would have become of Germany had there not been a power superior to that of this godless prince? It was Gregory VII who hurled him from his throne and restored to the noble Saxons and Thuringians their independence, not by the power of the sword, but by the scathing power of his anathema. The same I may say of Boniface VIII and of Innocent III. There was, happily for Europe, a Court of Appeal, to which even monarchs were forced to bow; and that court was Rome. It was to Rome that the nations appealed, when their independence was at stake, or their rights were trampled upon. And Rome was never deaf to the cry of distress, whether it came from Germany or from France, from England or from Poland, from Spain or from the shores of the Bosphorus.

The independence of religion from the control of the State a boon of which our constitution boasts was a thing for which the Popes, together with the bishops and priests, had fought and bled since the days of Constantino, and for which they gained the victory, centuries before America was discovered. The abolition of slavery was the constant aim of the Popes an aim which it accomplished without disturbing the harmony of nations, without wrenching in blood the countries where slavery existed; whereas, the powers succeeded in the abolition of slavery only at the cost of torrents of blood and millions of treasure, pressed out by merciless wars and political injustice. The cornerstone of society is Christian marriage; and at that cornerstone have the Popes, bishops and priests stood guard for eighteen centuries, by insisting that Christian marriage is one, holy, and indissoluble. Woman, weak and unprotected, has, as the history of the Church abundantly proves, found at Home that guaranty which was refused her by him who had sworn at the altar of God to love her, and to cherish her till death. Whereas, in the nations whom the Reformation of the 16th century tore from the bosom of the Church, the sacred laws of matrimony are trampled in the dust; whereas, the statistics of these nations hold up to the world the sad spectacle of divorces as numerous as marriages, of separations of husband from wife, and wife from husband, for the most trivial causes, thus granting to lust the widest margin of license, and legalizing concubinage and adultery; whereas, the 19th century records in its annals the existence of a community of licentious polygamists within the borders of one of the most civilized countries of the earth; we must yet see the decree emanating from Rome that would permit even a beggar to repudiate his lawful wife, in order to give his affections to an adulteress. And when the liberty of a nation was on the verge of destruction, and when emperors, and kings, and barons rode rough-shod over the rights, natural and vested, of their subjects, forgetting the sacred trust confided to them, became tyrants, when neither prosperity nor undivided liberty were secure from that rapacious grasp; when even the rights of conscience were set aside with impunity; it was the Popes of Rome who buckled on the armor of Justice, and humbled the pride of princes even if, as a consequence, they had to say, with a Gregory VII, "Dilexi Justitiam et odivi iniquitatem ; ideo morior in exilio."

Thus, the Popes, the bishops and the priests are the light of the world, the organ of the Holy Ghost. They announce the most beautiful, the most useful truths; they speak to encourage the good, to exhort the weak, and to convert the sinner. It is not in their own name that they speak; no, beloved brethren, it is in the name of God. They open the Book of books. They trace out for everyone his individual duties, to the monarchs as well as to their subjects, to the learned and the ignorant, to the rich and to the poor, to the just and to the sinner. To all they offer instruction, counsel, and hope. Sometimes they inveigh against crime, sometimes they encourage virtue; now they relate the sweet consolations of the just, and again they describe the fearful state of the impenitent sinner. There is not a sound maxim, nor a political truth, whose germ is not found in the Word of God. Now it is the Popes, the bishops, and the priests whom God has appointed to dispense these treasures. Yes, show me, if you can, a single country blessed by faith and civilization, which has not been watered by the tears and by the preaching, by the prayers and by the blood, of those who are styled the light of the world the Popes, the bishops, and priests.

Chapter 3

THEY ARE "THE SALT OF THE EARTH"

IF it is the Popes, the bishops and priests who have drawn forth the civilized nations of the world from barbarism, it is also the Popes, the bishops and priests who keep them from falling back into their former degradation. It is for this reason that our Divine Savior calls them also "the salt of the earth." Almighty God, who incessantly watches over the welfare of His Church, has, in every century, provided chosen vessels holy Popes, bishops and priests to defend and uphold her holy doctrine. Against Arianism, God raised up an Athanasius and a Hilary of Pointiers; to oppose the Nestorians, God sent St. Cyril. He sent St. Augustine to beat down the Pelagians; St. John Damascene, to fight the Iconoclasts. When the world became Christian, and Catholics grew rich, and forgot the poverty of our Lord Jesus Christ, the Franciscan monks were called to teach the love of Christian poverty to voluptuous Catholics.

Heresy and ignorance then followed, and the Dominican Fathers were raised up, by God, to combat these two great evils. In the

16th century, Protestantism came up. Heresy arose in all its strength: Luther was its ringleader and its spokesman; sensual passion and disobedience were personified in him. God raised up the Jesuit Fathers to oppose Protestantism, by self-denial, by an especial vow to the Holy See, and by their sound teachings of the Catholic religion.

Finally, in the 18th century, infidelity and impiety, the last consequences of Protestantism, personified in Voltaire and his associates, boldly raised their heads. Infidelity naturally united with Jansenism to undermine the edifice of the Church. Rigorism took hold of confessors and armed them with iron sternness against weak and shuddering sinners. The consequence was, that servile fear took the place of the charity of God; that the sacraments, the fountains of life, were abandoned, or turned into derision; that the Blessed Eucharist, the lifespring of Catholic piety, became an object of dread, and that the spirit of Christianity seemed to pass away. But the eye of an Omniscient Providence was watching over it. In order to confound impiety, to fight against Jansenism, to disarm confessors of their overstrained rigidity, to awaken faith, to kindle in the hearts of the faithful love for the Blessed Sacrament, God gave to his Church a man after His own heart, Alphonsus de Liguori. Infidelity had permeated society from the nobility to the lower classes, and the sons of St. Alphonsus, the Redemptorist Fathers, are preaching to the poor the eternal truths which they may have lost sight of by indifferentism and infidelity.

Truly, if the Church is the Spouse of Jesus Christ, the Popes, bishops, and priests are her guardians. If the Church is an army ranged in battle, the Popes, the bishops, and priests are her generals. If the Church is a vessel steering across the storms of persecutions, the Popes, the bishops, and priests are her pilots. If the Church is the Mystic Body of Christ, and if the faithful are its members, the Popes, the bishops, and priests are the principal members of this Body; by their eyes, Jesus

Christ watches over His flock; by their feet, He carries to every nation the Gospel of peace; by their hearts, He diffuses everywhere the life of that divine charity without which all is dead. If the Church is the people of acquisition, bought at a great price, the Popes, the bishops, and priests are the leaders, the teachers, the princes of that chosen generation. If the Church is that sacred edifice built up by the Divine Wisdom Itself for the children of God, the Popes, the bishops, and priests are the administrators of this palace; they are the columns of the Church upon which the entire world rests. God the Father has created the world without the Popes, the bishops, and priests, but it is only through them that He saves it. God the Son redeemed the world without the Popes, the bishops, and priests, but it is only by them that He applies His Blood to the souls of men and secures the fruits of His copious Redemption. And you can hardly name a single blessing of the Holy Ghost, without beholding by the side of that blessing the priest as the instrument through which that Divine Spirit communicates His blessing. Yes, if St. Bernard is right in saying that all comes to us through Mary, we are also right in saying that all comes to the people through the Popes, the bishops, and priests: yes, all happiness, every grace, every heavenly gift.

All the other gifts of God would avail us nothing without the Popes, the bishops, and priests. What would be the use of a house full of gold, if there were no one to open the door for you? Now the Popes, the bishops, and priests have the key to all the treasures of heaven; it is they who open the door. They are the stewards of the Lord, the administrators of His goods. Without them, the Passion of our Lord would profit us nothing. Look at the poor heathen of what benefit is our Lord's death to them? Alas! they can have no share in the Redemption, so long as they have no priests to apply His blood to their souls.

No one understands this better than the devil, and his associates in this world. When they wish to destroy religion, they begin by attacking the Popes, the bishops, and priests; for where there is no priest there is no sacrifice, and where there is no sacrifice there is no religion. What should we do in the Church? The people would say, there is no Mass now, our Lord is no longer there; we may as well pray at home.

Oh, how sad would be the state of society were the Popes, the bishops, and priests to be banished from the earth! The bonds that unite the husband and wife, the child and the parent, the friend and the friend, would be broken. Peace and justice would flee from the earth. Robbery, murder, hatred, lust, and all the other crimes condemned by the Gospel, would prevail. Faith would no longer elevate the souls of men to heaven. Hope, the sweet consoler of the afflicted, of the widow and the orphan, would flee away, and in her stead would reign black despair, terror, and suicide. Where would we find the sweet virtue of charity, if the Popes, the bishops, and priests were to disappear forever? Where would we find that charity which consoles the poor and forsaken, which lovingly dries the tears of the widow and the orphan; that charity which soothes the sick man in his sufferings, and binds up the wounds of the bleeding defender of his country? Where would we find that charity which casts a spark of divine fire into the hearts of so many religious, bidding them abandon home, friends, and everything that is near and dear to them in this world, to go among strangers, among savage tribes, and gain there, in return for their heroism, nothing but outrage, suffering and death? Where, I ask, would we find this charity, if the Popes, the bishops, and priests were to disappear forever? Leave a parish for many years without a priest, and the people thereof will become the blind victims of error, of superstition, and of all kinds of vices.

Show in an age, a country, a nation without priests, and I will show you an age, a country, a nation without morals, without virtue. Yes, if "Religion and Science, Liberty and Justice, Principle and Eight," are not empty sounds if they have a meaning, they owe their energetic existence in the world to the "salt of the earth" to the Popes, bishops, and priests.

CHAPTER 4

THEIR POWER OVER THE MYSTICAL BODY OF CHRIST

E VERY priest can say, in some measure, with Jesus Christ who sent him: "All power is given to me in heaven and on earth." The influence of this power is felt in heaven, in giving the elect; it is felt in hell, in snatching from it victims; it is felt in purgatory, in consoling efficaciously the Church Suffering. The influence of the priest's power is felt all over the world in sustaining the Church Militant. The great and the little, kings and their subjects, the learned and the ignorant, all expect from the priest not only the light of the true faith, but also pardon of their sins the grace of God. Indeed, the power of the priest is so great, that it can grant all these blessings in abundance. His power surpasses that of any created being, either in heaven or on earth. An earthly judge has great power, but, with all his power, he can only declare one innocent who has been falsely accused; but the priest has power to restore to innocence even those that are guilty.

The kings of the earth are powerful, yet their power extends only over a few countries, while the power of the priest extends over the whole earth. His power reaches to the highest heavens it penetrates even to the very gates of hell. The treasures of kings are silver and gold perishable metals, but the treasures of the priest are the imperishable merits and graces of our Lord Jesus Christ. Kings have power over only the bodies of men, but the priest has power over their souls. Kings have power over only their subjects, but kings and emperors themselves are subject to the priest. Kings have power to open and to close the prison-gates of earth, but the priest has power to open and to close the gates of heaven and of hell.

Yes, beloved brethren, this is no exaggeration. Listen to the words of our Lord Jesus Christ words which he addressed to his Apostles, and their successors in the priesthood: "I will give you the keys of the kingdom of heaven." Whatsoever you shall bind on earth, shall be bound also in heaven, and whatsoever you shall loose upon earth, shall be loosed also in heaven."

The priest is greater than the patriarchs, greater, more exalted, than the prophets. The widow of Sarepta fed the prophet Elias for some time. In reward for her charity, the prophet obtained for her the miracle that her pot of meal wasted not, and that her cruise of oil was not diminished, and thus sustained that family in a miraculous manner. The Catholic priest does more: he feeds not merely one family, but the entire human race; he gives not mere material bread, but the living bread from heaven the body and blood of Jesus Christ; he strengthens the souls of men with the oil of grace, which he administers to them in the Holy Sacraments.

Elias raised, moreover, the widow's son to life; but the priest does more: he raises to life the dead soul, not of one man, but of hundreds and thousands. In Baptism, and especially in the sacrament of Confession, he raises to the life of grace the souls of those that were dead in mortal sin.

Elias caused fire to rain from heaven upon the heads of the wicked. The priest causes not merely material fire to fall from heaven, he does far more: he causes the fire of divine love to fall upon the cold heart of the sinner and moves him to contrition; he inflames him to a new and perfect life.

Again, the priest is greater than the prophets. The prophets beheld the Redeemer only from afar, only in the dim future. The priest beholds Him present before his eyes. He touches the long-wished for Blessed Redeemer with his hands; he offers Him up to the Heavenly Father; he carries Him through the streets; he even feeds on the precious blood of this Holy One; he even receives Him into his heart and unites himself most intimately with Him in Holy Communion. The prophets foretold that when the fullness of time would come, God would write His law, not on stone, but on men's hearts. He would govern men, not by the law of servile fear, but by the sweet bonds of holy love; that God Himself would dwell in them and direct them by His grace. Now this fullness of time, for which the prophets sighed, has come.

God gives His grace, His own divine life to man, and He gives it abundantly; and as the ministers of this grace, he has chosen, not the prophets, not His angels, but His priests.

The Catholic priest has the primacy of Abel. Abel was hated and persecuted by his wicked brother; the priest is hated and persecuted by the wicked among his fellowmen.

The priest has the patriarchal dignity of Abraham. Abraham is called the Father of the Faithful. The priest is, in reality, the Father of the Faithful, for he makes them the children of God by preaching the Gospel, and especially by administering to them the Sacraments.

He stands at the helm of the Church, the ark of salvation, like Noah.

He is consecrated forever, according to the Order of Melchisedech.

He is invested with a dignity far higher than that of Aaron. Aaron offered up only the blood of sheep and oxen; the Catholic priest offers up the blood of the Lamb of God, our Lord Jesus Christ.

The priest has the authority of Moses. Moses led the people of God through the desert to the promised land; the Catholic priest leads the children of God through the desert of this life to the true Land of Promise our home in heaven.

The priest has the power of St. Peter, the power of the keys, the power of binding and loosing, the power of forgiving and of retaining sins. The priest has the power to free the sinner from the bonds of sin and hell, and to open to him the gates of heaven. He has the power to transform him from a slave of the devil to a child of God.

Let us take a man who, of his own free will, has made himself a slave of sin, a slave of the devil. Who shall free him from this shameful bondage? Shall we call upon the angels and saints of heaven? The saints of heaven are the friends of God, and God honors them by hearing their prayers. They may pray for the sinner, they may obtain for him innumerable graces, but they cannot free him from a single sin.

Shall we call upon his guardian-angel? The guardian-angel may warn the sinner, he may assist him, he may urge him to do penance, but the guardian-angel cannot free him from the chains of sin. Shall we call upon St. Michael? St. Michael is most powerful; he is the prince of the heavenly hosts; he has conquered Satan and his hellish crew. He can compel the evil spirits to flee away from the sinner, but he cannot free that sinner from a single sin.

Shall we, then, call upon the Blessed Virgin Mary herself? The Blessed Virgin Mary is the Mother of God; she is the Queen of angels and of men; her very name is the terror of hell. She can pray for the sinner, and her prayers are all-powerful with God, but she cannot forgive a single sin; no! not even a single venial sin.

Seek where you will, throughout heaven and earth, and you will find but one created being who can forgive the sinner, who can free him from the chains of sin and hell; and that extraordinary being is the priest, the Catholic priest." Who can forgive sins except God?" was the question which the Pharisees sneeringly asked." Who can forgive sins?" is the question which the Pharisees of the present day also ask; and I answer, there is a man on earth that can forgive sins, and that man is the Catholic priest.

Yes, beloved brethren, the priest not only declares that the sinner is forgiven, but he really forgives him. The priest raises his hand, he pronounces the words of absolution, and in an instant, quick as a flash of light, the chains of hell are burst asunder, and the sinner becomes a child of God. So great is the power of the priest, that the judgments of heaven itself are subject to his decision; the priest absolves on earth, and God absolves in heaven." Whatsoever thou shalt bind on earth shall be bound in heaven, and whatsoever thou shalt loose on earth shall be loosed also in heaven." These are the ever-memorable words which Jesus Christ addressed to the Apostles and to their successors in the priesthood.

Suppose that our Savior Himself were to come down from heaven and were to appear here in our midst; suppose He were to enter one of the confessionals, to hear confessions. Now let a priest enter another confessional for the same purpose. Suppose that two sinners go to confession, both equally well disposed, equally contrite. Let one of these go to the priest, and the other to our Savior Himself. Now our

Lord Jesus Christ says to the sinner that comes to Him, "I absolve thee from thy sins," and the priest says to the sinner that goes to him, "I absolve thee from thy sins." Now the absolution of the priest will be just as valid, just as powerful, as the absolution of Jesus Christ Himself. The sinner who goes to the priest to confession, will be just as well absolved as the sinner who goes to our blessed Lord Himself.

At the end of the world, Jesus Christ shall judge all men Himself; "for the Father judges no one, but He has left all judgment to His divine Son;" but as long as this world lasts, Jesus Christ has left all judgment to His priests. He has vested them with His own authority, with His own power. "He that heareth you,"

He says, "heareth Me." He has given them His own divine Spirit. "Receive ye the Holy Ghost; whosesoever sins you shall forgive, they are forgiven; and whosesoever sins you shall retain, they are retained."

The priest is the ambassador, the plenipotentiary, of God. He is the cooperator, the assistant, of God in the work of Redemption. Beloved brethren, this is no exaggeration, it is the inspired language of the Apostle: "Dei adjutores sumus." (1 Cor. iii.) "We are the cooperators, the assistants, of God." It is to the priest that God speaks, when He says: "Judge between Me and My people." "Judica inter Me et vineam meam." (Isa. v.) "This man," says God, speaking to the priest, "this man is a sinner; he has offended Me grievously; I could judge him Myself, but I leave this judgment to your decision. I shall forgive him as soon as you grant him forgiveness. He is My enemy, but I shall admit him to My friendship as soon as you declare him worthy. I shall open the gates of heaven to him as soon as you free him from the chains of sin and hell."

Great was the power and dignity of Joseph, the Viceroy of Egypt. From the prison, he was raised to the throne. From the rank of a slave, he was elevated to the first dignity in the kingdom. The King of Egypt took off his own ring and placed it upon the finger of Joseph. He clothed him in costly robes. He placed a chain of gold around his neck. He caused him to ascend into his second chariot, and commanded the herald to go before him to proclaim aloud that all should bend the knee before his viceroy Joseph. And the king said to Joseph: "Thou shalt rule over my house. Thy orders, my people shall obey; and without thy commands, no man shall move hand or foot in all the land of Egypt, and thou shalt be called the savior of the world." (Gen. xli. 40.)

Great indeed was the dignity to which Joseph was raised; but the dignity to which God has raised the priest, is infinitely greater. From the rank of a slave a vile slave of sin and hell God has elevated him to a dignity far surpassing that of the angels and saints of heaven. God has clothed the priest in the costly robe of grace and innocence. He has placed around his neck the golden chain of charity and mercy. He has placed on his finger the ring of power and authority. He has given the priest the almighty power of forgiving sins.

The priest has received from God the power of forgiving sins. But do you know, beloved brethren, what it means to have the power of forgiving, of destroying, sin? Sin is so great an evil, that were all the men on earth, were all the saints and angels of heaven to perform the most vigorous penances, were they to sacrifice everything for love of God, yet, with all their good works, they would not suffice to blot out a single sin. Nay, even the fierce fires of hell, though burning throughout all eternity, can never destroy a single mortal sin. To have the power of moving mountains is indeed something great; but to have the power of removing sin from the soul is something far greater. To have the power to raise the dead to life is wonderful; but the power to raise the dead soul to life is still more wonderful. To have the power to create new worlds, is to partake of God s own Omnipotence; but to have the power of forgiving, of destroying, sin, is to hold the very place of God

Himself it is to perform one of the greatest works of God's almighty power. Before concluding this point, I would wish to address a few words, in all charity, to those of my kind hearers who may not as yet be members of the Catholic Church.

There are many noble-hearted, precious souls; they are created by God for a high purpose created to shine amid the bright angels throughout all eternity. They are created with such keen sensibilities, that they seem born only to suffer and to weep. Their path to heaven is indeed a path of thorns. Their griefs and yearnings are such that, but few can understand them. God help these noble souls, if they are deprived of the strength and consolations of the Catholic Church out of the Church, such a gifted soul must bear her anguish alone. She was told, in the hour of happiness, that religion would console her in the hour of sorrow. And now her hour of sorrow has come. Whither shall she turn for strength and consolation? She turns to her books to her Bible.

But books are cold and wearisome; their words are dead. Oh, how she envies the penitent Magdalen, who could sit at Jesus' feet, and hear from His blessed lips the sweet words of pardon and peace! She turns to God in prayer; but God answers her not by the Urim and Thummim; and, in her doubt and loneliness, she envies even the Jews of old. Ah! she listens in vain for the voice of God because God has appointed a voice to answer her; but that voice is only within the shepherd's fold; and she is kept without the fold by the cruel enemy, and the shepherd s voice cannot reach her.

Ah, how different it is with the faithful Catholic soul! Try to call to mind some virtuous friend of your acquaintance; try to imagine one who is learned and pious, devoting his whole life, not to the care of a family, but solely to the service of God; imagine such a one ever ready to aid you in your necessities, spiritual and even temporal, ever wise in giving counsel, gentle in reproving, clear in teaching, and powerful in word and deed; imagine that such a one were your friend your intimate friend how great would be your happiness!

Imagine, moreover, that this kind, trustworthy friend, were appointed by God Himself to be your constant guide and director; imagine that he was bound by the most sacred oaths never to reveal, even by word or look, any secret you might confide to him; imagine, moreover, that this friend had received from God the power to forgive every sin that you confess to him with true contrition imagine all this, and you will have what every Catholic has in his confessor. The good Catholic is accustomed, even from his childhood, to communicate to his confessor every trial and temptation that disturbs his peace of heart. He goes to his confessor for consolation in the hour of darkness and sorrow; he asks his advice when in doubt; he consults him in every important undertaking. Our Lord Jesus Christ promised His beloved disciples that though He would quit the earth, yet He would not leave them "orphans," He would send them the Spirit of Truth to be their comforter. Now this divine promise has ratified, and even in a great measure fulfilled, when, on Easter Sunday night, Jesus appeared to His Apostles and gave them the Holy Ghost, saying: "Receive ye the Holy Ghost. Whosesoever sins you forgive, they are forgiven them, and whose soever sins you retain, they are retained."

On this solemn moment Jesus made His priests to be the fathers of the faithful, from whom they were to receive the spirit of grace and consolation, even to the end of time.

The same Divine Hand which poured such wonderful affection into the heart of the mother, fills the heart of the priest with divine charity, and teaches him to adapt his treatment to the spiritual wants of his penitent. The priest feels for his penitent as an earthly father feels for his child; and as a spiritual father, he judges and decides according as he thinks it is best for the eternal welfare of the penitent.

Ah! believe me, my dear Protestant friends, you cannot imagine the consolation, the peace of mind which a Catholic experiences when he has made a good confession; when he leaves the feet of the priest with the divine assurance which faith gives him, that his sins are really and truly forgiven. You cannot realize this joy by any force of the imagination. To understand this happiness, you must experience it as the Roman Catholic experiences it, who confesses with the infallible certainty that the priest has received from Christ the power to forgive sins.

The Episcopalian "Book of Common Prayer," at least in England, teaches that when one is sick and dying, he may have recourse to confession, and obtain the pardon of his sins, if his conscience be troubled with any weighty matter. The Catholic, however, needs not to wait until he is at the point of death, he can obtain the pardon of his sins whenever he desires it. He does not need to wait until his conscience is burdened by some grave matter, he can go to confession and obtain pardon for those daily sins and failings that vex the heart and weigh down the spirit by their frequent recurrence, even in spite of all our watchfulness.

To the faithful Catholic soul, the portals of the Catholic Church stand ever open. Hither she may come as to a healing fountain, whose waters ever flow. Here she may have her burning brow; here she may drink from the cooling stream and allay the feverish anguish of her soul. Here Jesus Himself, the dearest of friends, speaks to her by the mouth of him to whom He has given the Holy Ghost the spirit of consolation.

Mrs. Moore, a very intelligent lady of Edinton, N. Carolina, and a convert to our holy faith, said to her Protestant children on her deathbed: "O my children, there is such hope, such comfort in our holy religion! When I was so near death, and believed I should never see you again, my soul was filled with anguish. When I thought I was so soon to meet my God, I feared; but when I had made my confession to His own commissioned minister and received absolution in the name of the Holy Trinity, death was divested of every sting. Each day I thank God more and more that He has given me grace to break the ties that kept me from the Church. I have never looked back with regret, and, in fact, I wonder why I could ever have been anything but a Catholic."

CHAPTER 5

THE POWER OF THE PRIEST OVER CHRIST'S OWN BODY

G OD has given to the priest the keys of heaven. He has given the priest power over the faithful, over His mystic body; but He has given the priest even a more extraordinary power, a power so stupendous, so unutterably great, that, had we not the grace of faith, we could never believe it. He has given to the priest power over His own Sacred Body, power over Himself! The eternal, Omnipotent God, in whose presence the pillars of heaven tremble, that God before whom the earth, and all that dwell thereon, before whom the boundless universe, with all its countless suns and planets, before whom all created things are but as a drop of water, as a grain of dust, as if they were not; that God of infinite majesty and glory is subject to the priest. He instantly descends from heaven in obedience to the voice of His priest! The monarchs of the earth have great powers, their commands are obeyed, their very name is respected and feared. Thousands and thousands of their fellowmen are subject to them. Their power is great indeed, but there is no one on earth whose power is greater.

Great was the power of Adam when he came forth from the hands of God, in all the majesty of justice and innocence. He was king of creation, and all the creatures of the earth obeyed him.

Great was the power of Moses, when, by a single word, he divided the waters of the sea, and led a vast multitude dry-shod through the midst of the surging billows.

Great was the power of Elias, who caused fire to rain from heaven upon the heads of his enemies.

Great was the power of Joshua, who, in the heat of battle, raised his hands to heaven, and commanded the sun: "Move not, O sun!" he cried, "and thou moon, stand still;" and the sun and the moon obeyed his voice. They stood still in the midst of the heavens, for the space of an entire day!

Great, indeed, was the power which God thus gave to man, but there is one on earth to whom God has given power infinitely greater. There is a man who opens at will the gates of heaven, who speaks to the eternal Son of God, and at his voice the God of heaven descends on earth and subjects Himself to his control. We are astonished at the words of the Evangelist when he tells us that Jesus, the Son of God, was subject to Mary and Joseph. "Et erat subditus illia : and He was subject to them." But at least some reasons may be assigned to show the fitness of this obedience. Mary was the most pure and holy, the most perfect of God's creatures; she was the mother of God, and as such, had a certain right to the obedience of her Son; but when we see a weak, sinful man gifted with a power which angels dare not claim, when we see a weak, sinful man possessing power over God Himself, possessing power to bear Him, to place Him, to give Him to whom he wills, we cannot help exclaiming in amazement: "O wondrous miracle! O unheard-of power!"

And yet, beloved brethren, it is most true; we know it with all the certainty of faith. We are as certain of it as we are of the existence of God. There is a man on earth who possesses this extraordinary power, and that man is the Catholic priest!

The power which God has given to the priest is even far more excellent than the power of creation. By creation, God produces the substance of bread out of nothing, by His word; but by the words of the priest in consecration, the substance of bread is changed into the most Sacred Body and Blood of Jesus Christ.

So sublime is the dignity of the priesthood, that, in order to establish it, our Lord Jesus Christ had to die. To redeem the world, it was not necessary that our Lord should die. A single drop of His Sacred Blood, a single tear, a single prayer of His would have sufficed; but in order to establish the priesthood, our Lord had to die. He had to leave the priests of his holy religion a fitting sacrifice; he had to leave them a victim pure, holy, undefiled, worthy of God; and in the entire universe no victim could be found so worthy as Himself.

Hence our Lord Jesus Christ instituted, at the Last Supper, the sacrifice of His Sacred Body and Blood. On the night before His Passion, our Blessed Redeemer in presence of His Apostles, offered up bread and wine to His Heavenly Father; He then, by His almighty power, changed the bread and wine into His Sacred Body and Blood, and offered up His Body and Blood in sacrifice for our sins. "This," he said, "is my Blood, which is shed for the remission of sin."

He then empowered His Apostles to offer up this same Divine sacrifice. "Do this," He said, or sacrifice this, "in remembrance of me." It was, then, our Divine Savior Himself who first offered up the sacrifice of the New Law the sacrifice of His Body and Blood which we call the holy sacrifice of the Mass. The first Mass, then, that was ever celebrated on earth, was offered up by our Lord Jesus Christ Himself, at the Last Supper.

Now all good works together are not of equal value with the sacrifice of the Mass, because they are the works of men; but the holy Mass is the work of God. Martyrdom is nothing in comparison it is the sacrifice that man makes of his life to God; but the Mass is the Sacrifice that God makes of His Body and of His Blood for man. In this sacrifice there is nothing to be seen but the Infinite. The priest is God the victim is God. The holy sacrifice of Mass is essentially the very same as the sacrifice of the cross. It differs from the sacrifice of the cross only in appearance. On Mount Calvary, the victim offered to God was the living Body and Blood of our Lord Jesus Christ, and in the holy sacrifice of the Mass, the victim is also the living Body and Blood of our Lord Jesus Christ.

On Mount Calvary, the priest that offered the sacrifice was our Lord Jesus Christ Himself; and in the holy sacrifice of the Mass, the priest that offers sacrifice is also our Lord Jesus Christ.

On Mount Calvary, Jesus Christ was really and visibly present, and on the altar, during holy Mass, Jesus Christ is also really present, though invisible.

On the cross, our Savior died a painful and bloody death; but in the holy Mass, our Savior dies only in appearance, or, as it is called, a mystical death.

In the holy sacrifice of the Mass, the Body and Blood of our Lord Jesus Christ are not dead; no, it is the living Body, the living, warm heart's Blood; it is the living, rational soul of our Lord Jesus Christ, united to His Divinity, that are offered to God in the holy Mass. It is this which gives the holy Mass an infinite value, which makes it the highest worship that can ever be offered to God. In the holy Mass, the

Son of God worships His Heavenly Father for you; He prays for you; He asks pardon for you; He adores, He gives thanks for you.

What, then, must be the effects of this august sacrifice? God, appeased by the sacrifice of the Mass, forgives even the most enormous sins by granting to the sinner the grace of doing penance for them. Without doubt, it is to the efficacy of the Mass that we must attribute the less frequent occurrence, in later times, of those terrible punishments which God formerly inflicted on the wicked. "It is to the Mass," says Timothy of Jerusalem, "that the entire world owes its preservation; without it, the sins of men would have annihilated it long ago." (Orat. de Proph.)

Now the Catholic priest is the only one of God s creatures who can offer to Him the holy sacrifice of the Mass. It is by a single Mass that he gives God for you, and for all men, more honor, and more thanks, than all the angels and saints of heaven. It is by a single Mass that he obtains for you, and for all men, more blessings; that he averts from you, and from all men, more chastisements; that he appeases God more efficaciously than all the prayers of the angels and saints of heaven can do.

The priest's hands, more sacred than the cherubim that upheld the mercy-seat, more venerable than the sapphire throne on which appeared the Ancient of days, more blessed than even the spotless womb of the immaculate Virgin Mary his hands touch and handle the Incarnate Word of God. His hands bear that sacred Body, before whose dazzling splendor the angels veil their faces in trembling awe. Yes, at the altar I can imagine the blessed spirits in the attitude in which St. John the Evangelist beheld them. "They lay prostrate on their face before the Lamb of God." (Apoc. vii. 11.) But the priest is standing at the altar; his is the authority, and the action. The angels are only witnesses of the holy sacrifice, and God wills that the priest should be its minister. The angels are prostrated before the Lamb of God upon the altar, but the priest is at the table of the Divine Lamb; he incorporates Himself with Him Whom the angels hardly dare look upon. The holy Church, contemplating the unutterable privilege of the Blessed Mother of God, cries out in admiration; "O blessed is the womb of the Virgin Mary, which bore the Son of the Eternal God, and blessed are the breasts that suckled Christ our Lord!" But we can say, with even more justice: "O blessed, thrice blessed, are the hands of the priest into which the Eternal Son of God descends every day from heaven; blessed are those hands which bear, which handle, which sacrifice the ever-blessed Son of God I" The Son of God descended but once into the chaste womb of the Virgin Mary, but He descends every day into the hands of the priest.

Five words of her humility brought the Eternal Word into her sacred womb. Five words of the power of the priest bring the same Eternal Word upon the altar. If the consent which Mary gave was the conditional cause of the mystery of the Incarnation, speaking in the name, and in the all-powerful virtue of Jesus Christ, is the efficient cause of Transubstantiation the New Incarnation which is but an extension of the first. And what Mary did but once, the priest does every day. While she gave to the Son of God a life of suffering, which ended by the torment of the cross, the priest renders Him present, in his hands, in a state immortal and impassible.

Oh, beloved brethren! with whom shall I compare the priest? Next to God, his equal cannot be found, either in heaven or on earth. It is in establishing the priesthood that God seems to have exhausted all the treasures of His power and mercy. Indeed, in the light of faith, the man disappears altogether in the priest. Faith beholds in him nothing but Jesus Christ, continuing, in him and through him, the work of Redemption, for the honor of His Father and the salvation of mankind. Faith sees but Jesus Christ Himself in the priest when he preaches: "Go," says Jesus Christ to the priest, "as My Father has sent Me, so send I you. All power is given to Me in heaven and on earth. Go, therefore, teach all nations; he who heareth you, heareth Me."

Faith sees but Jesus Christ in the priest when he remits sin. The priest does not say: "Jesus Christ absolve thee;" no, he says: "I absolve thee."

Faith sees but Jesus Christ in the priest when he consecrates at Mass; for at the consecration the priest does not say: "This is Christ's Body" he says: "This is my Body."

Faith sees in the priest but the man of the Blessed Trinity. "Go," says Jesus Christ to the priest, "baptize all nations in the name of the Father, and of the Son, and of the Holy Ghost." The priest is the man of God the Father, to sustain His cause, to make His name respected, to defend His interests, to promote His glory, to vindicate His honor, to adopt for Him children, to prepare them for His service and His Kingdom.

The priest is the man of the Son of God; he is the preacher of His Gospel, the sacrificer of His Body, the dispenser of His mysteries, the treasurer of all His graces. The priest is the man of the Holy Ghost. He is His organ to enlighten the minds of men, to purify and sanctify their hearts, to establish and confirm in their souls a most intimate union with this Divine guest.

"I in them," says Jesus Christ of the priests, "and thou (Father) in me. The glory which thou hast given me, I have given them." (John 17, 22, 23.) Truly, "the priest," says St. Ambrose, "is a man all divine;" and the royal prophet says particularly of the priests, "Ye are gods."

To forgive sins, to cause the Holy Ghost to dwell in the soul, to change bread and wine into the body of God, are miracles that can be performed only by God Himself. Now the priests perform these miracles every day, and consequently they may be truly said to be gods; and St. Gregory Nazianzen is right in saying: "The priest is a God on earth, and his mission is to make gods of his fellowmen."

Next to God, the priest is everything. Truly the Catholic priest can only be understood in heaven. If we could understand him upon earth, we would die of love. What admiration and respect, what love and veneration, would be elicited for him whom the Lord would associate with Himself in the government of the universe, ruling, with him, the course of the stars, the vicissitudes of the seasons, and, add if you will, creating with him new worlds. Avocation so marvelous would place in a rank by itself this privileged mortal. But the priest is the object of a distinction far more glorious. He is not called, it is true, to direct the course of the sun, to excite or calm the winds all that is within the circle of nature and time. But the priest is called to give to heaven the elect, to snatch victims from hell, to sanctify souls, to concur in the redemption of a world, spiritual and indestructible, to fill the greatest of kingdoms with inhabitants all radiant with glory, divine and everlasting.

Since God, then, has placed the priest upon the throne of His own adorable sanctity, since He gives to the priest the title of "Savior of the World," since He calls the priest "His cooperator in the divine work of redemption," what wonder if He commands all to obey and honor the priest as they honor and obey Himself? "He that heareth you," He says to the priest, "heareth Me, and he that despiseth you, despiseth Me." "He that toucheth you, toucheth the apple of Mine eye." Since the priest has been so much honored by God Himself, what wonder is it that he should be honored by angels and men?

St. Francis de Sales saw the guardian angel of a young priest, whom he had ordained, go in advance to the right of the priest, before his ordination; but after his ordination, the angel went to the left of the priest and followed him. The Emperor Constantine, at the Council of Nice, sat last. Wenceslaus, King of Poland, would not sit down in the presence of a priest. St. Catharine of Sienna, and Mary of Oignies, kissed the ground on which a priest had walked. St. Francis of Assisi said that if he saw an angel from heaven, and a priest, he would first bow to the priest and then to the angel, for the angel is the friend of God, but the priest holds His place.

CHAPTER 6

THE CATHOLIC PRIEST IS THE FATHER AND FRIEND OF THE PEOPLE

G REAT, unutterably great, indeed, are the powers of the Catholic priest. But it is not merely as the celebrator of the rites of Divine worship; it is not merely as the minister of the sacraments; it is not merely as the preacher of God s Holy Word, that the Catholic priest stands conspicuous in the midst of his people. No, beloved brethren, he has not received his extraordinary powers for himself; he cannot absolve himself; he cannot administer the sacraments to himself; he lives not for himself; no, he lives for the people : he is the companion of their hardships, he is the soother of their afflictions, the guardian of their interests; he is the trustee of their hearts, the sentinel of their death-beds.

From his youth, the priest renounces the glory and honors of this world. He bids an eternal farewell to family pleasures, and to a thousand enjoyments that are permitted to others, in order to sacrifice himself freely for the good of his fellowmen: to be their father and best friend. The priest generally spends, previous to his ordination, from about ten to twelve years in hard studies, which often undermine the health and weary the mind. And for whose benefit is it that he undertakes so many difficult studies during the best part of his life?

It is for the benefit of the people; it is to enable himself to teach and guide aright, in the pathway to heaven, all those who will be placed under his spiritual direction. After his ordination, the priest spends all the days of his life in the service of his neighbor. On Sundays, you see him, for your temporal and spiritual welfare, at the altar, or in the pulpit, or in the confessional. On week-days you may see him, early in the morning, raising his hands to God, in prayer, in offering the atoning sacrifice for the people; and the man of charity the priest of God spends the remainder of the day in preparing his sermons, in instructing the children in school in their catechism, in relieving the poor, in visiting the sick, in wiping away the tears of the unfortunate, in causing the tears of repentance to flow, in instructing the ignorant, in strengthening the weak, and in encouraging the good in the practice of virtue.

Go through the streets of any of our cities or towns. Enter the hut of the poor. Ask them who gave them the alms that keep them from death and despair, and they will tell you that it was the priest, or some charitable soul guided by the zeal of the priest. Go to the sick bed; draw near the bedside of that poor wretch whom everyone has forsaken: ask him who is the consoling angel that pours upon his weary heart the balm of hope and consolation, and he will tell you it is the priest.

About twenty years ago, when the French troops were encamped around Gallipolis, the cholera burst suddenly upon them. They were unprepared for that terrible visitor. Father Gloriot, S. J., alone in an army of ten thousand men. "I was obliged," says he, "to hear their confessions on my knees, and stooping by their couches. Indeed, I learned then that to save souls for Jesus Christ it is necessary to undergo, with Him, the double agony of mind and body. Yet my greatest trial was my loneliness. I was alone; I had not had the consolation of confession for six weeks past; everybody died around me; and should I be taken sick, there was none to assist me in my dying hour. But God, in His mercy, preserved me, that I might attend to the wants of souls so well prepared. The trials were certainly great, but great were also the consolations. Whenever I entered those places of desolation I was hailed from all parts "Chaplain, here! Come here I to me! Make haste to reconcile me with God! I have only a few moments to live! Some would press my hand to their hearts, and say, with grateful feelings, how lucky for us that you are here! Were you not with us, who would console us in our last moments?"

Enter the dark and moldy dungeon where the unhappy prisoner pines away in weary captivity; ask him who it is that lightens his chains and makes his prison walls look less dreary, and he will tell you it is the priest.

Go upon the scaffold where the wretched criminal is about to expiate his crime. Who is it that stands at his side, and strips death of its terrors? It is again the priest. With one hand the priest shows the dying man the cross, the hope of the repentant sinner, and with the other he points to heaven, that blessed home where the weary find rest.

In 1851, the following murder was committed near Paris, in France: A captain of the carbineers, an excellent officer, be loved by all, going, as usual, the rounds of the stables, had reprimanded one of the troopers whose conduct had not been very regular. The latter made no reply, but turned away with apparently a calm countenance, and went up to the messroom. There he loaded one of his horse-pistols, and, going back to the stable, approached his captain, and, with a deadly aim, discharged the arm against the loins of the officer. The unfortunate man fell, weltering in blood. They had taken him up, carried him to his room, and the surgeons had pronounced the wound mortal. In fact, the poor captain had breathed his last in a few hours after, in the arms of his old mother, in the midst of horrible sufferings, endured heroically, and with sentiments of faith and charity truly admirable. He had made his confession with great piety, had received the Blessed Sacrament, and, in imitation of his Divine Master praying on the cross for His crucifiers, had pardoned his murderer, and begged for his pardon with the most touching and pressing appeal. The murderer had been arrested on the spot and transferred to a prison in Paris. There he was abandoned by all, except by the priest. Two or three days after the deed had been committed, the priest went to see the trooper for the first time in the cell of the military prison. He encouraged him to hope in the mercy of God, and to prepare himself for a good confession, and to accept death in expiation for his crime. The poor criminal was touched by the words of the priest and said: "I have been the victim of a moment of fury and insanity. It was a punishment from God, whom I had abandoned. Had I always prayed as I do now, I should not have come to this pass. My father said to me often: Fear God, and pray to Him; He alone is good, all the rest are nothing! But it is so hard to do so at the regiment; we are always surrounded by young men who say nothing but what is bad." When he heard that he was sentenced to death, he exclaimed: "The sentence is just; to appeal would be going against the goodness of God. They would show me a mercy that I do not wish for, because the punishment must be undergone. I must atone for what I have done. My hopes are no longer here below; I have only God now to look to. He is now everything to me; in Him alone do I trust; I feel quite calm; I feel no rebellion in my heart I am perfectly resigned to the will of God."

Now what brought about that calmness, that happiness, in this poor prisoner? It was his sincere confession, which the priest was kind enough to hear it was Holy Communion, which the priest brought to him several times in a word, it was the charity of the priest, who often went to see him in his prison, in order to console him, and to inspire him with great confidence in the mercy of God.

During the three hours and a half of the drive to the place of execution, he never lost his calmness God was with him in the person of the priest, who accompanied him to the Savory Plains, where he was to be shot. What a touching spectacle, to behold, on a wagon, a tall man the culprit followed by the priest of God to see how the priest was even paler than the culprit; and, to see them walking side by side, you would think that he was the one to be shot! The expression of the culprit's countenance was great calmness and resignation, his eyes betrayed at once sorrow and hope. He seemed to pray with fervor. There was no sadness in his looks there could even be seen the reflection of a certain inward joy. He listened with love, and deep attention, to the words addressed to him by the minister of Jesus Christ. When the priest said to him, "Our Lord is between us two, my poor child, we are always well when the good Savior is with us," he replied, "Oh, yes, my heart is perfectly happy; I did not think I should tell you, but I feel as if I was going to a wedding. God has permitted all this for my good, to save my soul. I feel so much consoled, thinking that my poor captain died so Christianly! I am going to see him; he is praying for me now. My God has saved me; I feel that He will have mercy on me. He ascended Calvary carrying His cross: I accompany Him. I shall not resist whatever they wish to do with me, tie me, or bandage my eyes. Ah! the poor soldiers are lost because they do not listen to you priests. Without you, without religion, the whole world would be lost!"

When they drove by the barracks, where he had committed the murder, he offered a prayer for his captain. "I can't conceive how I could do it! I had no ill- will against him! Could the commission of a sin save me from being shot, I would not do it; I think so now. I have nothing to keep me here, I am going to see God!" When they had arrived at the place of execution, the priest and the culprit alighted. An officer read the sentence. The culprit replied:" I acknowledge the justice of my punishment, I am sorry for what I have done, I beg of God to pardon me; I love Him with all my heart!" Then he knelt; the priest gave him the crucifix to kiss, for a last time. "My father," he said, with feeling expression," my father, I place my soul within your hands; I unite my death with that of my Savior, Jesus. Farewell! farewell!" The priest embraced him once more. Then, with his arms extended in the form of a cross, the culprit inclined his head, and awaited his death. The priest retires to pray at some distance. One minute after, human justice had been satisfied, and the soul of the unfortunate soldier, purified and transformed by religion, had fled to the bosom of Him who pardons all to those who repent. The priest resumed his place by him, and, with tears in his eyes, prayed, on his knees, for the departed soul of the unfortunate carbineer.

Ah! beloved brethren, go where you will, through all the miseries of this life, and you will find that everywhere the consoling angel, the father of the poor and friendless, is the priest; he labors day and night, without boasting, without praise, and often without any other reward, in this life, than contempt and ingratitude. If a dangerous disease breaks out in the parish, the priest does not abandon the post of danger. No, beloved brethren, the Catholic priest is no coward, the Catholic priest is no hireling. Devoted and fearless, he remains to encourage his flock, to give them the last sacraments, and, if need be, even to die with them.

A poor man is dying in his wretched hovel. In the midst of the winter's night the priest hears a knock at his door; he is told that one of his flock requires his assistance. The bleak winter wind howls around him, the chilling rain beats pitilessly in his face, yet he hurries on; there is a soul to save, there is a soul to aid in its fearful death-struggle; that makes him forget everything else. At last, he enters the house of death; he enters the sick man s room, though he knows that the very air of that room is loaded with pestilence. He receives the last whisper of the dying man; he breathes into his ear the sweet words of pardon and of peace. He bends over the sick man's infected body and breathes the tainted breath from his lips. The priest is willing to risk his own life provided he can save the soul of his fellowman.

During the Crimean War, cholera raged in the division of Herbillon. The soldiers became restless; they looked gloomy, and spoke despondingly, because the victims were many, and it was not the kind of death a soldier likes. What troubled the soldiers most was the prevailing thought that the plague was communicated by contact; and there was great dejection in camp. "What shall we do, Monsieur Abbe?" said the General to Father Parabere; "those boys look as if they were frightened." "O, it is necessary to let that fear know that it has to attack Frenchmen and Christians! leave it to me, General." And the dauntless priest walks straight to the very quarters where the pest raged most furiously. A poor soldier was in the last convulsions, and in the throes of his agony. The heroic priest had still time left to console and to absolve him, and then he closed his eyes. Then he called all the comrades of the dead man around his couch, and endeavored to persuade them that the scourge was not contagious; but as some of them shook their heads, he added, "You will not believe me to-day, you shall to-morrow." And just think of it, the brave priest lies down on the same couch with the man dead of cholera and prepares himself to pass the night with that novel bedfellow! Many hours passed away, and Pere Parabere, who certainly had worked enough during the day to need rest, did not quit his post until he was called to prepare another man for death. On the morrow, the whole camp had heard of it, and the soldiers, recovering from their fear, said to one another, "There's a man who has no fear!"

It is only a few years ago that a young Irish priest, then in the first year of his mission in this country, received what to him was literally the death-summons. He was lying ill in bed when the "sick call" reached his house, the pastor of the district being absent. The poor young priest did not hesitate a moment; no matter what the consequence to himself might be, the Catholic should not be without the consolations of religion. To the dismay of those who knew of his intention, and who remonstrated in vain against what to them appeared to be an act of madness, he started on his journey, a distance of thirty-six miles, which he accomplished on foot, in the midst of incessant rain. Ah I who can tell how often he paused involuntarily on that terrible march, or how he reeled and staggered as he approached its termination? Scarcely had he reached the sick man's bed, and performed the functions of the ministry, when he was conscious of his own approaching death; and there being no brother priest to minister to him in his last hour, he administered the viaticum to himself, and instantly sank on the floor, a corpse.

Ah, my beloved brethren, how often does not the priest risk his health, his honor, his life, and even his immortal soul, iii order to help a poor dying sinner I How often is not the priest found on the battle-field, whilst the bullets are whistling, and the shells are shrieking around him! How often is he not found on his knees beside the dying soldier, hearing his last confession, and whispering into his ear the sweet words of pardon and peace! How often must not the priest visit the plague-stricken in the hospitals, and in the wretched hovels of the poor! How often must he not remain, even for hours, in a closed room beside those infected with the most loathsome diseases! When all else, when friends and relatives, when the nearest and dearest have abandoned the poor dying wretch, then it is that only the priest of God can be found to assist him in his last and fearful struggle.

Whilst St. Charles Borromeo was Bishop of Milan, there broke out a fierce plague in that city. The priests of the city generously offered their services. They entered the houses of the plague-stricken; they heard their confessions and administered to them the last sacraments. Neither the loathsome disease, nor the fear of certain death, could appall them, and they all soon fell victims to their zeal. Death swept them away, but their places were filled by other generous priests, who hastened from the neighboring towns, and, in a short time, one thousand eight hundred priests fell victims to their charity. And not in Italy alone, in every clime beneath the sun, the Catholic priest has proved the earnestness of his charity by the generous sacrifice of his life. I need only remind you of the sufferings and heroism of the Catholic priests of Ireland, during the long and bloody persecutions that have afflicted that ill-fated country. Their sad, yet glorious, history is, no doubt, familiar to you all. The Catholic priests of Ireland were outlawed; they were commanded to quit the country; they were hunted down like wolves. But, for all that, they did not abandon their poor, suffering children. They laid aside their rich vestments, they laid aside their priestly dress, and disguised themselves in the poorest and most humble attire. Their churches were burned down and desecrated; but then the cabins of their persecuted countrymen were opened to them.

And the Catholic priest shared in the poverty and the sorrows of his poor children. He followed them into the forest: he descended with them into the caves. Often in some lonely hut, in the midst of a dreary bog, or amid the wild fastnesses of the rugged mountains, the priest could be found kneeling at the bed side of a poor, dying father or mother, whilst pale and starving children were weeping around. There you could find the Catholic priest hearing the last confession of that poor soul, aiding her in her death-struggle, and reciting the touching prayers of the church, by the dim flickering of a poor rushlight. The Catholic priest did not abandon his poor, persecuted flock, even though he knew that a price was set on his head, though he knew that spies and informers were in search of though he knew that well-trained bloodhounds were sent out to track him. The Catholic priest did not forsake his children, though he knew that if he were taken, the rack and the gibbet awaited him. He suffered not only poverty and sorrows with his poor flock, but he often underwent the cruelest death; for whenever a priest was found in the country, the tender mercy of the tyrant had decreed that he was to be hanged, drawn and quartered.

Ah, beloved brethren, would to God, I could take you to the Martyr's Room in Paris, where priests, loving their God and their neighbors, are incessantly preparing themselves to go to preach the Gospel, suffer and die for the faith, among the Pagans! Would to God you could see there that sacred army filled with generous soldiers of Jesus Christ, who aspire to the pacific conquest of infidel realms; who burn with the hopes of shedding their blood on the battle-fields of faith, sacrifice, and martyrdom; who very often attain, after a life of labors, toils, and torments, the ensanguined crown, which has been the goal of their life-long aspirations!

When they have attained it, when their head has fallen under a Pagan s sword, their vestments, their hallowed bones, the instruments of their martyrdom, are reverently gathered by the Christians of the lands where they have been martyred, and sent to Paris and the hall where all these precious relics are gathered is called the Martyr's Room. The sight alone of this sanctuary, fresh with the blood of those lovers of Jesus Christ, is the most eloquent of sermons on the priest s charity towards the people. Bones, and skeletons, and skulls of martyred priests enclosed in glass cases, instruments of martyrdom, paintings representing insufferable torments, iron chains which tortured the limbs of the confessors of faith, ropes which strangled them, crucifixes crimsoned with the blood of those who impressed on them their last kiss of love, garments, ensanguined linen O, what a sight! Great God, what a lesson!

Here a huge cangue, which rested for six long months on the shoulders of Bishop Borie, there a mat clogged with the blood of John Baptist Cornay, who upon it was beheaded and quartered, like the animal that is butchered. Nearby, a painting describing the horrible surplice of the blessed Marchant, whom the executioners chopped all alive, from head to foot, until he died of suffering and exhaustion. Everywhere, in every corner, the image of the good priest dying for the love of God and of his brethren, and of the fiend in human shape crucifying, with an indefatigable hatred, our Lord Jesus Christ, in the person of His priests.

Ah, if you wish to know what the Catholic priest has done, go ask the winds, that have heard his sighs and his prayers; ask the earth, that has drunk in his tears and his blood; go ask the ocean, that has witnessed his death-struggle whilst speeding on an errand of mercy! Go to the dreary shores of the icy north, go to the burning sands of the distant south, and the bleached and scattered bones of the Catholic priest will tell you how earnestly he has labored for the welfare of his fellowmen.

Ah, beloved brethren in Christ, could the many happy souls that have died in the arms, died with the blessing of the priest, could they appear before you at this moment, ah! they would describe to you, in glowing language, the great benefits they have derived from the Catholic priest. They would say to you "We were weak and helpless, but the consoling words of the priest gave us strength. We trembled at the thought of God's judgments; but the blessing and absolution of the priest gave us a supernatural courage. We were tormented by the assaults of the devil; but the power of the priest put the evil one to flight. We were heartbroken at the thought of bidding a long farewell to wife and children, to the nearest and dearest; but the priest turned our weeping eyes towards a happier home, where there is no parting, no weeping, no mourning, anymore! And even when our soul had left the body, when our friends were shedding fruitless tears over the cold corpse, even then the priest of God still followed us with his prayers; he commended us to the mercy of God; he called upon the angels and saints to come to our aid to present us before the throne of God. Ah! now we understand, indeed, that whosoever sins the priest forgives on earth, they are truly forgiven them in heaven."

The priest has enemies. He knows it, but he does not complain. The world, too, hated and persecuted his Divine Master. But the priest opens his lips only to pray for them; he raises his hand only to bless them. He remembers the words of Jesus: "I say to you, love your enemies, do good to those that hate you, bless those that curse you, and pray for those that persecute and calumniate you"; and, like his Divine Master, the priest says: "Father, forgive them."

During the French Revolution, a wicked monster, who had often dyed his hands in the blood of priests, fell dangerously ill. He had sworn that no priest should ever set his foot in his house, and that, if any dared to enter, he should never leave it alive. A priest heard of his illness; he heard, too, of the impious vow he had made. But he heeded it not. The good shepherd must be ready to lay down his life for his sheep. As soon as this wicked monster saw the priest standing before him, he flew into a rage: "What!" cried he, "a priest in my house! Bring me my pistols." Then the dying ruffian raised his brawny arm and shook it threateningly at the priest. "See!" he cried, with a horrible oath, with this arm has murdered twelve of such as you." "Not so, my good friend," answered the priest, calmly, "you have murdered only eleven. The twelfth now stands before you." Then baring his breast, he said: "See here, on my breast, the marks of your fury! See here the scars that your hand has made! God has preserved my life, that I might save your soul." With these words the priest threw his arms around the neck of the dying murderer, and, with tears in his eyes, conjured him, by the precious Blood of Jesus Christ, to have pity on his poor soul, and make his peace with God.

Such, my beloved brethren, such is the Catholic priest. I tell the truth when I say that he is indeed an angel of God, with the heart of a man.

CHAPTER 7

OBLIGATIONS OF THE PEOPLE TO THE CATHOLIC PRIEST

BEFORE concluding this little work, I must speak of another point of great importance. Holy Scripture tells us, that, when the holy man Tobias considered the great benefits which God had bestowed upon his family through the angel Raphael, he was seized with fear; he was at a loss how to express his gratitude; he and his family fell prostrate upon their faces for three hours, thanking and blessing the Lord. He called his son Tobias, and said to him: "What can we give to this holy man that is come with thee?" And the young Tobias said to his father: "Father, what wages shall we give him, or what can be worthy of his benefits? He conducted me and brought me safe again; he received the money of Gabelus, he caused me to have my wife, and he chased from her the evil spirit; he gave joy to her parents, myself he delivered from being devoured by the fish, thee also he hath made to see the light of heaven, and we are filled with all good things through him. What can we give him sufficient for these things? But I beseech thee, my father, to desire him that he would vouchsafe to accept of half of all the things that have been brought." (Tobias, chap. xii.) It is thus, my beloved brethren, that this holy family showed themselves thankful to God and His holy angel for the divine blessings.

Now you have heard that the priest is, for you, the true angel of God; you have heard that his dignity is far more sublime than that of the angel Raphael; you have heard that the priest's powers far surpass those of all the angels of heaven; you have heard that his offices are of greater importance to you than those of the angels; you have heard that the benefits which God bestows upon you through the hands of the priest, far surpass those which He bestows through His holy angels; you have heard that the Catholic priest lives not for himself, but exclusively for you; that he is invested with the most extraordinary powers, not for his benefit, but for yours; in a word, you have heard that God has given you, in the priest, all the goods and blessings of heaven and earth. What fitting thanks can you, then, offer to him? Ah! if the Lord had only once shown you but one single mark of affection, even then you would be under infinite obligations to Him, and He would deserve an infinite thanksgiving from you, inasmuch as that affection is the gift and favor of an Infinite God. But since you daily receive, through the priest, blessings of God, infinite in number and greatness, what should then be your thanksgivings to God and His angel the priest? With Tobias you should say:" What shall we give to this holy man? What can be worthy of his benefits?" Were you, in imitation of Tobias to offer to God and His priest one-half of all your goods, it would be a poor return for the Divine blessings.

Believe me, you will never be able, in this world, fully to understand what God has given to you in the priest, and what you should be to the priest; you will understand it only in the world to come. But let me beseech you to believe, at least, what you cannot understand. And if you live up to this belief, you will listen to our Lord when He speaks of the priest, and says: "He that receiveth you, receiveth Me, and he that receiveth Me, receiveth Him that sent Me." (Matt. x. 41.) Our Divine Savior spoke these words to His Apostles and to all priests in general, to encourage them in establishing on earth His kingdom the Catholic Church. You know very well, that in order to establish and keep established the holy Church, the priests have to announce the Gospel truths; they have to administer the Sacraments. But this is not enough: they have also to build churches, or keep the old ones, and everything that belongs to them, in good condition and repair; they have to erect and to support Catholic schools, hospitals, and orphan asylums. They are the ministers of God, and as such, they are charged with the honor of His worship, and the care of His sacred temples. They are, moreover, the almoners of the poor, and the fathers of the needy. How, think you, can poor priests meet all the expenses that they must necessarily incur in the exercise of the sacred ministry? Only put yourselves a day or two in the place of your priests: take care of all the poor of the place; assist all the needy that come to your door, or that modestly hide their poverty from everyone but the priest of God. Try to support Catholic schools, colleges, hospitals, orphan asylums. Build new churches or keep old ones in good condition. Do all this, and more, and you will find out what the difficulties and crosses, the troubles and hardships of the priests are in this country. You will find out that it requires heroic virtue, angelic patience, and superhuman courage in the priests, to comply with their duties towards God and men.

Jesus Christ knew full well all the difficulties which His poor priests had to encounter. But He encourages them. He says to them, "He that receiveth you, receiveth Me; and he that receiveth Me, receiveth

Him that sent Me. He that receiveth a prophet (a priest) shall receive the reward of a prophet of a priest. Jesus Christ made the salvation of the people dependent on the priest, and He made also the priest dependent on the people for his support and other expenses which he has to incur in the exercise of the sacred ministry. It is by this mutual dependence that our divine Savior has the priests united with the people. The devil the cursed spirit of discord has often tried to break up this sacred union between Catholic nations and their clergy. He has succeeded in many countries by means of Protestant governments, but he never could succeed in one country in the country of the glorious St. Patrick, in Ireland. There the perfidious government of England offered, not long ago, to support the Catholic clergy. Had this offer been accepted, the Catholic priests of Ireland would have become dependent on the English government, and that close union and warm love, that deep-rooted respect and esteem, which, for so many centuries, has existed between the Irish Catholics and their priests, would soon have fallen a prey to the devilish trick of a perfidious government. But thanks be to God, and to the foresight and wisdom of the Irish clergy, the devil, and his Colleagues- the English government met, in, this instance, as in many others, with a cold reception with a flat refusal.

Jesus Christ has given to His priests ever so many reasons to keep up mutual love between themselves and the people. Priests, no doubt, will do all in their power to establish and to preserve this love. But Jesus Christ wishes also that the people should preserve this mutual love between themselves and the clergy. To obtain this object, they are commanded to support and assist the clergy; but in order to make them observe this commandment joyfully, Jesus Christ holds out to the people a most powerful inducement. He says to every Catholic: "If you receive my priest, you receive Me; and by receiving Me, you receive my Heavenly Father." In other words, Jesus Christ says that, by supporting and assisting the priests, you support and assist your Divine Savior Himself, who looks upon all the difficulties of His priests as His own, because they are His representatives on earth.

Moreover, in order to make Catholics cling to their priests, and keep them closely united with them, Jesus Christ promises them an immense reward. He says: "He that receiveth a prophet, (a priest) shall receive the reward of a prophet." Our Divine Savior has attached great blessings to the charity which is shown to the least of His brethren on earth. "Amen, I say to you, as long as you did it to one of these, my least brethren, you did it to Me." (Matt. xxv. 40.) By saying "to the least of these, My brethren," Jesus Christ gives us to understand that there is another class of His brethren who are great in His sight, and whom He loves most tenderly. Now, if God bestows such great blessings upon those who are charitable to the least of the brethren of Jesus Christ, how much more abundantly will He not bestow His blessings upon those who are charitable to His great friends? The Holy Ghost calls our particular attention to this great truth when He says in Holy Scripture: "If thou do good, know to whom thou does it, and there shall be much thanks for thy good deeds. Do good to the just, and thou shalt find great recompense, and if not of him, assuredly of the Lord." (Eccles. xii. 1, 2.) To the just, especially to those of them who are eminently so, may be applied what the Angel of the Lord said of John the Baptist, namely, that "he was great before God." (Luke i. 15.) The reason of this is, because Jesus Christ lives in the just by His grace. "I live, now not I," says St. Paul, "but Christ liveth in me." (Gal. ii. 20.) Hence, whatever is given to a just man is given to Christ Himself in a more special manner. To show this in reality, Christ has often appeared in the form and clothing of a poor man, and as such begged and received alms. This happened to John the Deacon, as is related in his life by St. Gregory. The same saint relates also (Hom.

39, in Evang.), that Jesus Christ, in the form of a leper, appeared to a certain charitable monk, named Martyrius, who carried Him on his shoulders. The same happened to St. Christopher, also to St. Martin, Bishop of Tours. When he was still a soldier, and receiving instruction for admission into the Catholic Church, he gave one-half of his mantle to a poor man; the following night Jesus Christ appeared to him, wearing this mantle, and said to the angels who surrounded Him: "Behold, this is Martin, who gave Me this mantle!"

Once St. Catherine of Sienna gave to a poor beggar the silver cross she wore, having nothing else about her to give. During the night Christ appeared to her, and said that, on the Day of Judgment, He would show that cross to the whole world in proof of her charity. God, then, rewards liberally those who are charitable to the least of His brethren; but He rewards far more liberally all those who are charitable to His friends to the just. "He that receiveth a just man," says Jesus Christ, "in the name of a just man (that is, because he is a just man, a friend of God), shall receive the reward of a just man."

But what will be the reward of all those who liberally and joyfully support and aid the priests the ministers and true representatives of God through whose ministry men are made just and holy? To understand this, I must make here a very important remark, to which I call your special attention: namely, that there are degrees in this well-doing. The more just a man is, both for himself and others, the more souls he leads to justice, to holiness of life, the greater will be his reward, and consequently the greater also will be the reward of him who assists such a just man. "They that instruct many to justice, shall shine as stars for all eternity." (Dan. xii. 3.) To whom can these words of Holy Scripture be applied more truly than to fervent pastors of souls and missionary priests? They devote their whole life to the salvation of souls. Now there is nothing more pleasing in the sight of God than laboring for the salvation of souls. "We cannot offer any sacrifice to God," says St. Gregory, "which is equal to that of the zeal for the salvation of souls." "This zeal and labor for the salvation of men," says St. John Chrysostom, "is of so great a merit before God, that to give up all our goods to the poor, or to spend our whole life in the exercise of all sorts of austerities, cannot equal the merit of this labor."

This merit of laboring in the vineyard of the Lord is something far greater than the working of miracles. To be employed in this blessed labor is even more pleasing to the Divine Majesty than to suffer martyrdom." If, then, in the opinion of the Fathers of the Church and all the saints, there can be no greater honor and no greater merit than that of working for the salvation of souls, we must also say that there can be no work of corporal mercy more honorable and more meritorious than that of giving charitable aid to the pastors of souls, to missionary priests, and to persons consecrated to God. To such as give this aid may be applied the words of the prophet: "They shall shine as stars for all eternity." "The charity which you bestow," says Aristotle (Lib. I. Ethic, c. 3), "will be so much the more divine, the more it tends to the common welfare." But what kind of charity is tending more to the common welfare than that which is bestowed upon such apostolic laborers as spend their life exclusively in laboring for the salvation of souls? Now this charity is divine in a most eminent degree, and consequently it makes all those divine who bestow it. They shall, without doubt, shine as the stars, nay, even as the sun, throughout all eternity." Then the just shall shine as the sun in the kingdom of their Father" (Matt. xiii. 43); and this glory and happiness of theirs in heaven will be in proportion to the zeal and fervor with which they have continued to furnish charitable aid to Jesus Christ, in the persons of the ministers of the holy Catholic Church. "He that receiveth a prophet, shall have the reward of a prophet." He who receives a prophet, says our Lord, that is, he who gives charitable aid to a priest, will receive the reward of a priest. The reason of this is, because by his charitable aid he contributes towards the spreading of the Gospel, and, therefore, as he thus shares in the labor and in the merits of the Gospel, he must also share in the reward promised to the true minister of God. Should you aid a man in performing sinful actions, you would become accessory to his sins. So, in like manner, by assisting the priests with a cheerful heart. When God, in His bounty, vouchsafes to call you to cooperate in any of His works, he does not employ soldiers, or tax-gatherers, or constables to collect the impost He accepts from you only a voluntary assistance. The Master of the Universe repudiates constraint, for He is the God of free souls; he does not consent to receive anything which is not spontaneous and offered with a cheerful heart.

To conclude: The Catholic priest is the priest of the Lord of heaven and earth; impossible for you to conceive a higher dignity!

The Catholic priest is the plenipotentiary of God; impossible for you to conceive a greater power!

The Catholic priest is the minister of God; impossible for you to conceive an office more sublime and more important!

The Catholic priest is the representative of God; impossible for you to conceive a higher commission!

The Catholic priest is the vicegerent of God; impossible for you to conceive a higher merit!

The Catholic priest is the treasurer of God; impossible for you to conceive a greater benefactor of mankind, a man worthier of your love and veneration, of your charity and liberality!

May you, therefore, my beloved brethren, always receive the priest as the Galatians received St. Paul the Apostle. "You despised me not," writes this great Apostle to the Galatians, "you did not reject me, but you received me as an angel of God, even as Christ Jesus. I bear you witness that, if it could be done, you would have plucked out your own eyes, and would have given them to me." (Chap. iv. 14, 15.)

www.ingramcontent.com/pod-product-compliance
Lightning Source LLC
Chambersburg PA
CBHW070936120626
46546CB00004B/1428